TUGBOATS

William Burt

MBI Publishing Company

Acknowledgments

Thanks to all the people at Crescent Towing, David Cooper, Prentiss (Tadd) Wilcutt, Captain Joe Tucker, Captain Mike Yarbrough, Tom Lambard, the crews of the *Alabama*, the *Ervin S. Cooper*, and the *Mardi Gras*, and last but not least, David Richards.

First published in 2000 by MBI Publishing Company, 729 Prospect Avenue, PO Box 1, Osceola, WI 54020-0001 USA

The information in this book is true and complete to the best of our knowledge. All recommendations are made without any guarantee on the part of the author or Publisher, who also disclaim any liability incurred in connection with the use of this data or specific details.

We recognize that some words, model names and designations, for example, mentioned herein are the property of the trademark holder. We use them for identification purposes only. This is not an official publication.

MBI Publishing Company books are also available at discounts in bulk quantity for industrial or sales-promotional use. For details write to Special Sales Manager at Motorbooks International Wholesalers & Distributors, 729 Prospect Avenue, PO Box 1, Osceola, WI 54020-0001 USA.

Library of Congress Cataloging-in-Publication Data Available

ISBN 0-7603-0824-1

On the front cover: The most simple tugs on the water today are the "single screw boats." A large diesel engine provides nearly 1,500 horsepower to drive an 8- to 10-foot propeller. Without these simple, powerful tugboats, mammoth ships would be unable to maneuver in the close quarters of today's ports.

On the frontispiece: When one hears the term "tugboat," the endearing image that most comes to mind is that of a harbor tug. The image of the tugboat is one that lasted for generations. Of the 3,726 tugboats listed as U.S. Flag Vessels as of December 31, 1996, only 153 were less than 5 years old, while 2,277 were more than 20 years old.

On the title page: Maneuvering large ships into harbor often requires more than one tug. Tugboat companies often send more than one boat to control a ship; in this case, the sister ships *Jim Colle* and *Kimberly Colle*. The combined horsepower of the two tugs will surpass 3,000—more than enough for the ensuing ballet of coaxing a 100,000-ton ship to berth.

On the back cover: Tugboats come in many different, job-specific configurations. While the general design of an oceangoing tugboat is the same as a harbor tug, these specialized ships move large deep-sea barges *across* the oceans. When at sea, the barge is pulled with a cable about 200 feet behind the tug. Only when the barge enters harbor, does an oceangoing tug assume the more traditional role of pushing its payload.

Edited by John Adams-Graf
Designed by Dan Perry

Printed in China

Contents

Preface

I once read that if the human immune system would remain as strong as it is at age 16 throughout our lives, then our bodies could hold out for about 800 years. Obviously, a life span of that length could have many advantages, one of which would be the opportunity to master many professions—a prospect that with our limited time we can only dream of. High on *my* list would be tugboat captain. Operating a tugboat is a job that consists of performing the same task over and over, yet no two jobs are the same. I can watch a tugboat work with the same appreciation and fulfillment of senses that an art expert receives from gazing at a beautiful painting. I love the working smell of diesel fuel, the comfortable roar of the engines, and the look of a vessel that has all of the charm and grace of a bulldozer, yet remains a maneuverable and romantic vessel.

I normally write about automobile racing, but when my editor, John Adams-Graf, mentioned that he was looking for a writer to compile a book on tugboats, I jumped at the chance, much to John's surprise. Over the next few minutes, in tentative voices, we both confessed that we liked tugboats but did not know why. In a blinding moment of clarity, he said that tugboats are "honest" vessels. I liked that. Tugboats are like rugby players: what you see is what you get. They work. They don't mind it. They roll up their sleeves and get in close. They know that damage to their bodies is inevitable, but like offensive linemen, calmly accept it as part of the job. And in a day when most marine designs (whether it be a 25-foot sailboat or a 400-foot cruise ship) are built with the same sharp lines, white paint, and tinted windows, the tugboats plow along with their vertical lines, bright paint, and used tractor tires hanging over the side. Tugboats are salty. I can see Popeye taking the helm of a tugboat, but I'll be damned if I can see him conning the *Love Boat*. Very few things in the world today are what they seem to be. Most products and many people are dressed up to be something that they are not. But not tugboats. There is no room for anything on a tugboat unless it positively affects the performance of the boat or crew. Tugboats tend to be the smallest boat fitted around the largest engine, with the most minimal superstructure. Their job is to push, pull, and control with no fluff.

Likewise, the crews of the tugboats provoke interest, from the deck hands throwing and checking lines to the captain standing his lonely vigil in the small pilothouse. It is tough work, but free on the water. The steady roar of the diesels keeps you company, and the beautiful views just keep drifting by. Some crews are home by nightfall; others stay out for days on end pushing the cargoes of the nation around the clock. While it is a difficult, time-consuming, and often lonely job, to the people trapped in offices it takes on an air of romance and adventure, attributes that are often missing in the careers that we choose.

The purpose of this book is to give the reader an overview of the primary types of tugboats and their activities, and to give a "tour" of an operating tugboat. It will also present a fundamental picture of tugboat techniques, and will expose the reader to some of the language and terms used in the world of tugging.

It would be impossible in a text this size to cover all types of tugs, and as result, broad generalities are often, regrettably, required.

CHAPTER ONE

A Brief History of Tugboats and Tugging

While the modern tugboat is the product of mechanical engines (first steam and then diesel), the art of tugging has been around for hundreds of years. Ship assist, or moving ships about in close quarters, was once left to rowboats, either carried by sailing ships or hired in the harbor. This often dictated the size of the sailing ships themselves. Larger ships could be built, but if they were too large to be sailed from or pulled into port, they would be useless as freighters. At best, they would require offshore unloading, a costly and dangerous practice. It is indeed the harbor tugboats that have allowed the existence of huge modern ships and efficient port facilities.

Waterborne barge traffic has also been around for many centuries. Pulled by mules, barges transported goods and people through canals for many years in many countries. In fact, the tractors that today pull ships through

Nothing on the waterfront matches the sight of, or stirs emotions like, a tugboat. They are the street fighters of our country's ports, rivers, and waterways. Their tough and simple form is perfectly matched to the heavy work that they perform.

A pushboat and its barges continue their lonely trek down the Mississippi River. Barging has long been an integral part of the American commerce system. Before good roads were available, rivers were the best means of transporting goods to market.

the Panama Canal are still called mules, referring back to the days when the ships were pulled through the locks by mule teams.

Most agree that the modern tugboat can be traced to Scottish engineer William Symington, who in 1802 fitted a steam-powered paddle wheel to a boat for the purpose of efficiently pulling barges up and down canals. The first test of this craft was successful; however, it was the only job the boat would accomplish. Canal authorities feared that the huge wake produced by the craft would erode the sides of the canals. But Symington had proved that barges could, and would, be propelled by auxiliary power. Barges would first

be pulled on towlines and later pushed by steam-powered tugs.

Powered ship-assist tugging also has its roots in Britain. In 1814 the *Perseverance*, a steam paddleboat, was completed for passenger transport. Within a few years the company that owned her went out of business, and the *Perseverance* was sold. The new owner, feeling the pinch of the competitive passenger trade, was always looking to make a quick buck. He offered, for a fee, to pull a sailing ship from port to open sea. Much to the relief of the men who were standing by to pull the ship out to sea with rowboats, a deal was struck and the ship was towed from port in record time. Such

America's waterways are as crowded as they have ever been. Tug captains must share the water with ships, barges, and thousands of recreational boaters.

was the birth of modern ship-assist commercial towing.

The early tugboats were all steam powered. Most were fitted with a single, relatively low-horsepower steam engine driving two side paddlewheels. Compared to modern tugs, these early tugs were underpowered and difficult to steer and maneuver. Later, the single steam engine was replaced with a two-engine setup, with each engine independently powering a side paddlewheel. Not only did this increase power, but the design allowed the captain to run one paddlewheel ahead and one in reverse for turning purposes. As a result, these were the first

tugs that could turn completely around within their own length. This dramatic increase in maneuverability was a great advantage for the tugboat captains. It allowed them much more control, letting them put their tugboat exactly where they wanted it and keep it there.

By the mid-1800s, experiments into the new technology of the screw propeller were taking place. At the forefront of this technology was a Swedish engineer, John Ericson. At this time the screw propeller had one problem: it was new. It was a much better system than the side paddlewheels, but it was slow to be accepted, especially by the British who,

perhaps averse to change, kept building the paddlewheel tugs. In fact, the British continued to build paddlewheel tugs clear into the 1900s, but for the rest of the world the writing was on the wall. By the late 1800s, the propeller had begun to replace the side-paddlewheel arrangement.

It was during this period that another major change took place. The reciprocating steam engine was fitted into tugboats. These engines had much more power than the early single-stage steam engines. This dramatically increased the engine power of the tugboats, with no real increase in overall size.

While more reliable, and very powerful for their time, the reciprocating steam engines still had problems. They required large crews. A tugboat needed three crew members just to run the engine. Just like steam locomotives, a steam tug had a fireman, a boiler, and an engineer. The engine controls were not by the helm, but in the engine room. Thus, the captain had to relay commands from the pilothouse to the engine room through speaking tubes or by whistle signals. As the engines themselves had poor throttle response (they took a while to speed up or to slow down), the increased communication time for engine commands greatly affected the captain's ability to quickly maneuver the tugboat. Early steam engines were also very heavy and bulky for the amount of power they produced.

Without tugboats, the use of mammoth ships would be impossible. While these ships safely sail the open oceans, they are cumbersome and not nearly maneuverable enough to navigate crowded ports and dock on their own. Only with the assistance of tugboats can they load and unload their cargoes.

Today's tugboat industry consists of three major types: harbor tugs (above), which assist ships in tight quarters; oceangoing tugs (opposite, top), which assist disabled ships in deep ocean and pull large open-water barges; and pushboats (opposite, bottom), which are used to propel and steer barges.

While tugboat equipment has changed over the decades, the men who operate the boats have kept their individuality and their sense of humor. Here a captain shows off his new pilothouse companion. It is said that this captain's previous pet was an orangutan, who when passing would occasionally sit at the controls. Needless to say, this brought some stares from the other boaters.

The stage was set for another great breakthrough in tugging, and two came in the early 1900s: steel hulls and diesel engines.

Even today, when complex modern materials are common, many commercial lobster and shrimp fishermen prefer wood boats. And while it can still be strongly argued that wood is the best boat-building material in existence, for tugboats it is not. For a craft designed to be in controlled impacts all of its life (and most likely a few uncontrolled ones as well), the toughness of steel was a great benefit. This allowed boats to last longer and be less susceptible to hull damage during their long lives. It allowed tugboat captains to push harder without as much worry. And pushing harder

became a reality with the introduction of the diesel engine.

Just as it did for locomotives, the diesel engine forever changed tugboats. The three-man engine crews could be cut to just an engineer, with a great cost saving for the owner. And tugboats became much more powerful. Diesel engines seemed to offer everything—better control, better throttle response, a smaller (less expensive) crew, and a much better horsepower-to-weight ratio. One diesel tug could now do the work of two or three of the less powerful steam tugs.

While these were great technological advances, some captains who remember the steam tugboats still miss them. One of the biggest differences in the boats is noise. Steam tugboats were relatively quiet, and diesel boats are pretty loud. Hearing protection is mandatory in diesel engine rooms. Even so, the diesel age had pretty much taken over by the 1930s, and while a few steamboats were still on the water in the late 1940s and early 1950s, no more were built. The few that remain today are either rusted hulks or beautifully restored museum pieces.

From this time in the 1930s until fairly recently, the general design of the tugs stayed the same. However, in layout and equipment they have changed dramatically. Engines have been refined to be small, light, and efficient, yet provide more and more horsepower. Power plants were increased from one diesel engine to two or more. Propellers with variable-pitch control (just like airplanes) were developed for tugs. Propellers were then enclosed in Kort nozzles to greatly increase forward thrust. Z-drives were invented, allowing the entire propeller to pivot 360 degrees

The modern tugboat uses technologies at both ends of the spectrum. On the low-tech end they use steel, chains, old tires, and rope. On the other end are modern, efficient engines and high-tech electronics such as radar and satellite communications. *Mack Burt*

for incredible control and maneuverability. Next, these Z-drives were arranged with one located forward and one aft, giving birth to the tractor tug, a boat that can theoretically push from the side as well as the bow. Recently, the Voith-Schneider system was developed: it eliminates screw propellers altogether by using spinning discs with independently controllable vanes extending downward, for propulsion and control. During the ensuing 70 years, advances were also made in safety, training, electronics, pilothouse design, and hull design. The results are modern vessels that look more like spaceships than tugboats.

Yet through it all, the job has remained constant. To push, to pull, and to assist. Perhaps the best description of a tugboat came from the tug captain who said, "It is a vessel between 80 and 120 feet in length and of 700 to 4,000 horsepower. It may have a Kort nozzle, and may have flanking rudders. However, there is one sure way that you can tell if it is a harbor tug: the mast will be bent and the visor around the wheelhouse will be dented."

CHAPTER TWO

Modern Tugboats

Regardless of type, the tugboat fleet of the United States is an integral part of our country's commerce system, and in times of war a critical part of our defense. It allows for efficient use of the country's waterways, whether it be moving products in barges, helping dock larger vessels, or providing rescue and assistance to other mariners. The fundamental art of tugging has remained much the same since its inception; however, the boats themselves have changed dramatically.

Since many tugboats have been built to accomplish a specific task, it would be impossible in a text this size to discuss all of the types and sizes. As result, some broad generalities must be used. This chapter will discuss three primary categories of tugboats: harbor tugs, oceangoing tugs, and pushboats. Each does just what its name implies. Pushboats push

The harbor tug's primary duty is ship assist. Modern ships are far too large to maneuver on their own in restricted waters and are difficult, if not impossible, to dock on their own. Whether freighters or tankers, to accomplish these tasks they must rely on one or more tugboats.

Tugboats help the ships maneuver in tight channels, tie up when coming into port (docking), and leave port (sailing). To accomplish the task of moving objects so large, the harbor tug relies on strength and maneuverability. Compared to the ships that they move, tugboats' engines, rudders, and propellers are proportionately quite large for towing, handling, and pushing power.

barges. They are usually attached to the stern (back) of a single barge or a barge assembly and act as engine and rudder. Oceangoing tugs are some of the biggest tugboats around and handle large loads in the open ocean, where rough water can be expected. Harbor tugs work in the ports and harbors of the world, helping ships maneuver in close quarters. This may be docking (coming into port to dock), sailing (leaving the dock in order to sail

to another port), or assisting a ship in an especially crowded or narrow waterway.

Within each category the characteristics of the individual ships may range greatly in age, size, configuration, and performance capabilities. All tugs are built to the parameters of the specific jobs for which they are intended. They are a wonderful example of form following function. Many of today's vehicles don't enjoy the same luxury. From military jets to sailboats,

While every boat is different, the classic harbor tug is usually from 100 to 120 feet in length. Few tugboats would win a beauty contest. However, their "no-nonsense" look makes them one of the most popular boats to watch. In the days of modern design, where everything is sleek, shiny, and lookalike, a tugboat is one of the few "salty" craft still in existence.

most are built along lines of compromise, allowing them to do more than one task. For example, the traits that would allow a certain military jet to be a great air-to-air fighter may be abandoned so that the aircraft can be merely a good fighter as well as a good ground-attack craft. Tugboats are likely to be true to

their cause, with all design focused on accomplishing a single task.

Harbor Tugs

Whether it is nudging a shipload of sunburned tourists up to a dock or trying to move a burning freighter away from dock, the harbor

tug's duty is *ship assist*. These are the boats that pop to mind when most of us think of the classic tugboat. Their assistance allows larger, more cumbersome ships to be maneuvered with great precision and a high degree of safety in tight ports and channels. The harbor tugs' working attributes are toughness, power, maneuverability, and response. They are interesting machines. They must have the brute force of a bull but must operate with the precision and grace of a hummingbird.

Tugboats are the toughest boats seen on the waterfront. They have to be. The average 100-foot-long harbor tug will spend its life banging into ships that are often over 10 times its own length. Most of these impacts will be controlled accurately by the captain. Undoubtedly, a few will not. It is their inherent toughness that allows the tugboats to survive in this environment. But harbor tugs not only survive in this "impact rich environment"—they thrive. Harbor tugs exhibit great longevity. Of the 3,726 tugboats listed as U.S. flag vessels as of December 31, 1996, only 153 are less than 5 years old, while 2,277 are over 20 years old.

Size and power of harbor tugs differ greatly. Ship assist tugboats are usually 80 to 120 feet long. Power output may range from less than 2,000 horsepower to over 5,000. The drive systems come in many configurations.

The simplest tug, the "single-screw boat," has a large diesel engine providing power to a

Tugboats are relatively narrow for their length. This width-to-length ratio gives a tugboat excellent maneuverability, a must when dancing around large ships.

Harbor tugs ride low in the water, especially in the stern. Their hulls extend deep below the waterline so the huge propellers can get a good bite in the water. Without this bite, tugboats would find it difficult to make headway when pushing a 90,000-ton ship.

23

A tug may work with many different types of ships in a single day. Freighters and tankers of all sizes are the most common clients. Other jobs may include maneuvering work platforms, large barges, and oil rigs. Here a harbor tug assists a Chevron tanker to the dock. Cargoes are often hazardous, and an accident can mean either loss of life or terrible damage to the environment. As a result, tug captains are good and do not get an opportunity to take the helm until they are qualified with both experience and testing.

very large single propeller. Single-engine tugs will usually have around 1,500 horsepower driving an 8- to 10-foot-diameter propeller. Most of the tugboats with this arrangement are older boats that, due to their toughness, are still working the waterfront. Even though it is the simplest and oldest layout, some captains prefer these boats. Their advantages are simplicity and lower maintenance, and they are usually the least expensive boats to operate. A ship does not know if it is being docked by a 40-year-old single-screw boat that is paid for, or by a new multi-million-dollar boat that has really big monthly payments. The disadvantages of the single-screw boats are lower power output and less maneuverability than other types of tugs. If a single-screw boat is to turn around quickly, the captain must "back and fill." This means the captain will alternate coming ahead with the wheel turned all the way to one side and then going astern with the wheel turned the other way. It is a slow method compared to the turning performance of newer boats. When backing, a single-screw tug will be easier to turn in one direction than the other, due to the torque effect of the spinning propeller.

One job for which the single screw boat is still preferred is submarine assist. A twin-screw boat, with its propellers set to the outside of the keel, is much more likely to damage a round submarine hull than a single-screw boat whose propeller is set directly in the center of the keel.

The next type of propulsion arrangement is the twin-engine/twin-propeller boat. These boats have been taking over from the single-screw boats for many years. (It takes a long time because the single-engine boats take so long to die). The main advantages of this very common layout are more total power and much greater maneuverability. These boats make standard tugboat techniques much easier for the captain to execute. For instance, a tugboat position that is very helpful when docking a ship is keeping the tug's bow on the ship's side at a 90 degree angle. A twin-screw boat can do this maneuver more efficiently, as the captain can keep the angle steady by working

The modern ship-docking module is a radical departure from the conventional tugboat. With a different propulsion configuration and a more symmetrical hull, these boats handle far differently than their more conventional cousins.

A harbor tug's hull typically has a reasonably high bow but has very little freeboard in the stern. This means that in rough weather the boat will most likely take water over the side. To release this water, the sides and stern of the boat have large scuppers, which are openings at the edge of the deck that allow the water to flow back into the sea.

the port and starboard engines separately. A single-screw boat must either back and fill, which takes time, or press the tug's bow against the ship to pivot under power, which will move the ship (possibly when the ship does not need to be moved). Nor do twin-screw boats have the handling problems associated with propeller torque, because their propellers rotate in opposite directions, which cancels out the torque. Twin-engine boats may also continue to maneuver if one of the engines experiences a failure. One interesting point should be kept in mind when comparing single-screw

Tugboat companies keep docks in or around the waters where they work. While at the dock, the crew rests, eats, or works on the boat. The sea is a killer, and a harbor tug's life span is dependent on the amount of care that it receives.

Opposite: The pilothouse on a ship-docking module more closely resembles an airport control tower than the bridge of a tugboat. These pilothouses afford the captain unobstructed vision for a full 360 degrees.

and twin-screw boats. On tugboats of equal total engine horsepower, the single-screw boat will have greater pushing power because the single-screw arrangement (with the propeller on the centerline) is about 20 percent more efficient than the offset propeller layout of twin screw boats.

There are other propulsion enhancements that can be used on both single-engine/single-screw and twin-engine/twin-propeller boats. One of these is the Kort nozzle, a circular airfoil-shaped ring that fits closely around the outside diameter of the propeller. The effect of the nozzle is so great that it may increase the forward thrust of the propeller by up to 40 percent.

Another giant leap in power and control was made when the propellers were mounted so that they could pivot. Tugboats with these systems not only generate thrust with their propellers; they steer with them as well. Often referred to as "Z-drives," these systems work much like an outboard motor, except they can rotate a full 360 degrees. As a result, tugboats fitted with Z-drives can generally go backward

A harbor tug works up close and personal. The typical ship is much, much heavier than the tug, so if the tug is to survive it must be heavily protected. This means a very thick, reinforced hull and as many fenders as is possible.

A tugboat ties up to a barge waiting for the job to commence. The schedule usually consists of waiting or hurrying up.

While much like harbor tugs, the oceangoing tug is built on a larger scale. From hull size to engine power, everything is more, more, more. These boats are often used in salvage and rescue operations, which means there is a pretty good chance that boat and crew will be in some pretty bad weather.

The rear deck of an oceangoing tug shows the large steel guides and rollers used to keep the towline under control.

as well as forward, can pull in any direction, and can change the angle of their pull very quickly. All of these are a great advantage when assisting a ship.

The next step up in the evolution of tugboat propulsion is the tractor tug. They are named tractor tugs because their main function is pulling, and they have been cleverly modified to be very efficient at this function. The primary difference between tractor tugs and conventional tugs is the location and placement of the propellers. One or, in some cases, both of the propellers have been moved forward of the center of the boat. This gives the boat a mechanical advantage when pulling and also makes pulling a ship much safer by reducing the risk of capsizing. By moving one Z-drive forward and keeping one in the stern, the result is the nautical equivalent of four-wheel drive.

As oceangoing tugboats often operate with large loads in rough conditions, their hulls are heavily fendered. Collisions at sea are bound to occur, so impact resistance is critical. Both old tires and old nylon lines are converted to fenders to protect the hull. It may not be pretty, but it works.

While the general design of an oceangoing tug is the same as a harbor tug, everything is larger. The pilothouse sports large masts so the proper light and flag signals can be displayed. Different signal schemes indicate everything from the tug's direction to what it is towing.

The final type of propulsion used in tugging is the recent development of the Voith-Schneider propellers. Instead of using conventional propellers, these drive units use horizontal spinning discs with vertical vanes extending downward. While very efficient and powerful, these systems are more expensive to build and to operate than more traditional types of tugboat propulsion.

While each type of design has advantages and disadvantages, it is important to remember that the ship being assisted does not care what is assisting her, as long as the job is done correctly and within a reasonable time frame. Older boats are simpler and usually less expensive to operate. If they can do the job, then they will be the most economical choice for a tugboat company. After all, the tugboat business is like any other in which price less cost equals profit, and lower costs always help. It is also important to remember that tugboats are much like airplanes and race cars. A great captain with a mediocre boat will always outmaneuver a mediocre captain with a great boat.

Oceangoing Tugboats

The biggest and most powerful tugboats afloat are the oceangoing variety. While the hull designs for pushboats and harbor tugs make them optimal platforms for their particular jobs, they—especially pushboats—are not designed to operate in environments where high seas can be expected. That's not to say that they don't go to sea. With modern weather monitoring services, these tugs can make short runs into the open ocean. However, the sea is unpredictable, and any tug that will consistently be in the open ocean must be built to endure the worst weather situations possible. Oceangoing tugboats are built tough. Their power and the ability to operate in the deep ocean gives them two primary roles in maritime commerce: ship rescue and towing large, deep-sea barges.

When large ships, from freighters to aircraft carriers, lose power or rudder control at sea, they will most likely require assistance getting back to port. It takes a lot of boat to tow these craft. As a result, oceangoing tugs may exceed 200 feet in length and have four engines with a combined strength of over 20,000 horsepower. When trouble starts, an oceangoing tug will be dispatched to the crippled ship, which is often in the middle of the ocean. (Ships, like cars, will almost always break down at the worst time and in the worst place.) When the tug arrives, a line will be passed from the bow of the ship to the stern of the tugboat. This can often be a feat in and of itself. High wind, large unpredictable waves, pitching decks, and a great difference in deck height make this difficult and dangerous work. A tug captain must also be very wary of collision during such maneuvers. One wrong move can mean a collision, which can mean disaster, usually for the smaller tugboat. Once the towline has been secured,

An oceangoing tugboat comes into port pulling a large deep-sea barge. These barges are much more seaworthy than their river-traveling counterparts. When at sea, the barge is pulled behind the tug with a cable at a distance of several hundred feet.

While they push instead of tug, pushboats are commonly referred to as tugboats. Although considered by some to be the least romantic of tugs, the pushboat is an incredibly valuable contributor to American commerce. Every year pushboats silently move millions of tons of cargo at a very low cost.

While a harbor tug holds the barge in position, the oceangoing tug pulls into the notch. The notch is a recess in the stern of the barge into which the bow of the oceangoing tug will fit. Once this connecting maneuver is complete, the barge-tugboat combination reacts much like a conventional ship. This comes in handy when going through restricted waterways.

the tugboat will begin pulling the ship to port, where the harbor tugs can assist the ship into a regular berth or dry dock for repairs.

Oceangoing tugs may also be called to assist in pulling ships off when they become grounded. While grounding a ship is easy, getting it off can be difficult. Those in charge of "ungrounding" the ship must analyze many factors. The type of bottom on which the ship is grounded makes a difference. It takes more force to pull a ship off of a rock or coral bottom than from a sandy bottom. The tide schedule must be known. Using the tide is the easiest way to float the ship, and it may be practical to wait for a high tide, even if it means waiting for a few months. Ships that are aground may offload cargo to lighten the ship, although this can be costly and with some cargoes impossible.

Even though they are built to push barges, a pushboat can be handy around a port. Here a pushboat helps pin a grain barge to the dock while lines are taken loose for sailing.

Mariners have used the next option, beach gear, for hundreds of years. Beach gear usually consists of heavy cables, chains, and anchors. A cable is attached to the ship and run to the anchor, which is secured well away from the ship. Then, by using winches, the ship tries to pull free. Because of the awesome bulk of many modern ships, more than one set of beach gear may be necessary to move them. If all of these methods fail, a tugboat may be the last option.

Modern oceangoing tugs have the horsepower that 50 years ago mariners only dreamed of. When pulling a ship off, it is a real test of horsepower and thrust, as the tug sits in place and tries to pull thousands of tons of dead weight. A tugboat does have an advantage over beach gear. A set anchor can only pull in one direction, while a tugboat can easily change its angle of pull. By doing this, a tug captain can wiggle the ship or pull the vessel from side to side, helping break the suction between the bottom and the ship.

Pulling on grounded ships is also a test of the lines. Some types of line, especially steel cables, if broken while under load, will recoil like a whip back into the tugboat. The crews must always be cognizant of this, as a broken line can go in any direction and can literally cut a man in half.

When pulling on grounded ships or moving other large structures, more than one tug will be used. Teams of tugboats will combine their efforts in order to have more pulling power and better control. The tugs can pull in different directions for pinpoint accuracy.

Opposite: Although solid, strong, and powerful, pushboats are not suitable for rough water. Their boxy hull shape and low freeboard make the pushboat well suited to push, but not to riding out a storm. As a result, their activities are limited to rivers, bays, and other waterways that are either well protected or where cover is close at hand in case a storm blows up.

During these maneuvers the individual tug captains must communicate constantly so that each knows what the others are doing. Often five or more boats are used to keep control on such an unwieldy tow.

The second role of oceangoing tugs is much less romantic but still very important. They regularly pull large seagoing barges from port to port. These coastal barges may be over 600 feet in length and may carry anything from general cargo to oil and petroleum products. They differ from traditional river barges in that they have a V-type bow and much more freeboard (the distance from the water to the top of the hull). This makes them much more seaworthy than traditional barges.

When tugs are working with these large barges, they have two choices in how they can hook up. The barges can either be pulled or pushed. A cable and chain line, run approximately 100 to 150 feet behind the tug, will pull the barge when the tug and barge are in open water. As the tug comes into the ship channel, the barge will be hauled in closer to the tug for better control. As the tug enters even more confined waters, the pulling gear is disconnected and the tug moves to the rear of the barge to "set up in the notch." Most large oceangoing barges have a large notch in the stern so that a tug can slip her bow into it and

The bigger the load, the bigger the pushboat. Small pushboats can maneuver barges through small waterways, while huge pushboats can work in large rivers such as the Mississippi. Large bumpers at the front of the pushboat butt against the back of the barge. The pushboats' and barges' square shape allows for a solid fit.

Steel cables are used to secure the barge to the pushboat. The fit must be right. Any looseness will increase wear and stress on the hardware, and it will be more likely to fail.

hook up. This notch allows a very secure connection between tug and barge. When attached to the stern of the tug, the barge appears and handles like a conventional ship. During this hookup maneuver the oceangoing tug will most likely be assisted by a harbor tug, which will hold the barge steady while the oceangoing tug changes positions.

Pushboats

Next to rolling cargo down a hill, pushboats and barges are probably the most efficient way to move materials in the history of mankind. These relatively simple craft outperform any other means of transportation. Their cargo ranges from the mundane, such as wood chips, to the exotic, such as rockets for NASA. For cargoes such as the latter, barges may be the only option to move large structures over long distances.

As its name implies, a pushboat pushes. It is basically an engine and rudder for single barges or barge assemblies. These assemblies are often massive, hauling more than the super ships that ply the oceans. If you live within range of a navigable river, you have probably

Large pushboats may look like small buildings going down a river. With four engines, large fuel tanks, living quarters, and the control areas, the square footage adds up. While a pushboat may look peaceful as it glides down the river, the captain rarely has time to relax. The river is fraught with danger to his craft. Bridges, shallows, and other watercraft keep the captain busy.

The square shapes used in barging allow for great flexibility. Not only are loads easy to assemble, but docking can be much easier too. When a pushboat needs to tie up, the captain can simply slide in next to another barge and secure.

seen pushboats plying the waterways with some type of bulk cargo. In Alabama, it is usually coal being transported from mine to power plant or imports going north from the Port of Mobile. Pusher tugs are one of the reasons prices in the United States are so low on many items. It is the most economic form of shipping available.

Not only are pushboats very economical, they are versatile. While the big pushboats can guide colossal loads along the coasts and up and down the great rivers, smaller pushboats can weave small barge assemblies or even single barges through many of our nation's smaller rivers and waterways. This often allows for shipping to a port close to the cargo's final destination, eliminating costly overland hauling.

Small utility pushboats are also used to maneuver work and support barges. When building bridges and other structures on the water, barges make great work platforms. They may be used in bringing oversized parts to the workplace, or they may serve as platforms for cranes and other construction equipment. Small pushboats are used to move these barges into and around the workplace.

Some of the largest loads afloat are guided by pushboats. The amount of cargo pushed by one boat can become staggering. Barge assemblies can exceed 1,000 feet, with some reaching 1,200 feet. They can carry loads greater than most freighters in the world. To push these

Pushboats and barges are not used only for moving cargo. Small pushboats are often used to move working barges around construction sites. Building bridges, dredging, and working on ships are all made easier by the flexibility that these small boats provide.

41

A barge captain's view is always changing, from uninhabited wilderness to large cities. Life on a pushboat assures that a person will not become bored with the scenery.

colossal loads, colossal pushboats have been built. Some pushboats are up to 200 feet long and have over 10,000 horsepower.

The barge-pushboat combinations offer other advantages. They are relatively inexpensive compared to internally powered ships, and they draw less water, so they can be docked and sailed in much shallower water. Where a freighter may draw 30 feet when loaded, a loaded barge may draw only 10. And like railroad cars, an individual barge or a section of a barge assembly can be dropped off at a dock quickly, allowing the barge assembly to sail on and not have to wait on unloading. This

saves in docking costs and allows the pushboat to be on the water making money instead of at the dock costing money.

Barge assemblies may consist of 40 or more individual barges. All of these must be fastened together, or the whole assembly may be in danger of breaking up. Even if a single barge breaks free, it will be a hazard to navigation until it either runs aground or is retrieved by another tug. This happened in Mobile in the mid-1990s. The men of the Port of Mobile awoke to find a herd of barges, over 100 strong (some of Mobile's captains still say *thousands*) that had broken free and were taking a leisurely

Open barges are used to transport bulk cargoes that are not damaged by weather. These may include coal, gravel, metals, or wood chips.

float to the sea. One tug captain remarked that he could have stepped from barge to barge and walked across the port without getting his feet wet. The entire tugboat population, pushboats and harbor tugs alike, spent a hectic day rounding them up. No serious damage was done, and, interestingly enough, there was no charge to the owner of the barges. It is an unwritten rule of the waterfront that mariners do not take advantage of other mariners when they have problems. In times of emergency, the men of the waterfront work together with a sense of honor now unfortunately rare in this era of trial lawyers.

Maneuvering a pushboat is just as rigorous as maneuvering a harbor tug. Captains face many hazards. Wind and current both greatly affect the handling of a barge/pushboat assembly. Winding rivers mean constant course changes. The deepest channel of a river may change from bank to bank. When a captain stands at the wheel he must gauge the wind speed and direction and anticipate which way it will blow the craft. He must understand how hard and in what direction the current will move the craft and how deep the water is under the entire width and length of the vessel. And finally, he must be able to predict how all

Covered barges are used to allow perishable cargoes some protection from the elements. Cargoes such as grain can be moved without fear of the cargo getting wet and spoiling.

of these factors will work to his advantage or disadvantage during the tight 90 degree turn he is about to execute.

While pushboats are versatile craft, they are not extremely seaworthy in rough weather, especially when they are not hooked up to barges. Their flat, square hull design does not weather well, and often pushboats have very high pilothouses, giving the craft an extremely high center of gravity. A pushboat captain must know the mechanical condition of all of the barges and the pushboat. He must watch out for other commercial and recreational traffic, be aware of all obstructions, from bridges to floating logs, and be able to do all of this in rain, fog, or the dead of night. And he must be 100 percent correct. A mistake can mean disaster.

Many barge cargoes are very hazardous and if spilled will mean an environmental disaster. When craft of this size and mass are involved in collisions with other craft, bridges, and other obstructions, the result will most likely include injury and death.

Barges

Barge size ranges from tens of feet to hundreds of feet. Different types of barges have been developed, depending on what cargo is being moved and the environment in which it is being moved. The lower, flatter river-type barges are used in shallow and calm water. They are not seaworthy enough to risk open oceans with any type of wave activity. They will only venture out in very calm conditions, and a

Liquids as well as solids are moved by barges, many of which have double-hull construction. If the outer hull is punctured, the inner hull keeps the water out of the cargo.

captain must always keep an eye on the chart, looking for a safe harbor to run to in case some bad weather brews up.

Liquid cargo barges often carry dangerous cargoes and are usually of double-hull construction. This allows the outer plate of the barge to be punctured without fear of the barge sinking or the cargo being released. Some liquid cargo tank barges can be up to 300 feet long with a total capacity of around 1 million gallons. Common cargoes include petroleum, petroleum products such as diesel and lubricating oils, fertilizers, and other industrial chemicals. They may also carry consumables such as orange juice.

Open dry-cargo barges carry solid loads that cannot be spoiled by rain. Their 200-foot length allows for a 1,500-ton (3 million-pound) capacity. They may carry coal, steel and aluminum products, various ores, sand, gravel, or lumber.

Oversized barges can be custom-built to transport cargo. Everything from livestock to space shuttle components are moved by barge.

A special type of barge is the floating dry dock. These platforms can be moved into position by a tug and flooded. Then a ship is docked inside, the water pumped out, and presto—a huge ship is out of the water and ready to be repaired.

This is a gas station that will come to you. Fuel barges are a convenient way to fill up on the waterfront. A weekly visit by a fuel barge allows the tug operator to concentrate on business rather than finding fuel.

Covered dry-cargo barges are also up to 200 feet long, with a 1,500-ton capacity. They are the great link in transporting raw food goods from farm to market. They carry grain, soybeans, coffee, salt, sugar, paper products, and packaged goods.

There are a few options in how a pushboat is made fast to a barge or barge assembly. On a simple rectangular barge with a flat stern, the tug will usually attach in the center of the stern of the barge with heavy steel cables. Another option is pushing from "the hip" or being "hipped up," used when a tugboat is attached in a side-to-side configuration.

Most of the loads transported by barge are those that lend themselves to bulk shipment. Each year, around 256 million tons of petroleum and petroleum products are transported by barge. This is about a third of all cargo shipped by barge. Coal is next, at

Whether it is a ship repair or building a bridge, barges make wonderful platforms for cranes.

208 million tons. This accounts for a fourth of all barge loads moved in the United States. Other common loads for barges include materials such as wood and lumber, sand, gravel, stone, metals, grain, and other grain products. Also included in this list are industrial chemicals, sulfur, fertilizer, and paper products. Oversized and cumbersome cargoes that cannot easily be shipped by other means are often moved on open deck barges. In the past these have included nuclear reactors, drilling platforms, and even space shuttles. The pushboat and barge industry is critical in transporting equipment and supplies for the military, supporting the armed forces in peace, and in every major conflict of the past century.

While many consider the pushboats and barges less glamorous than their harbor tug cousins, their job is no easier nor less important. Their low cost of operation keeps product transportation costs and selling prices low. While accidents have occurred, the industry as a whole has an exemplary safety record.

CHAPTER THREE

Aboard a Tugboat

Tugboats have been described as the biggest engine surrounded by the smallest boat. While this may be somewhat true, by the average weekend boater's standards tugboats are not small. Harbor tugs usually range from 80 to 110 feet, and large oceangoing tugs often exceed 200 feet. Hull design, the arrangement of the towing equipment, and the general layout of the boat vary depending on the task the boat is built for, but almost all tugboats have the same basic compartments: engine room, pilothouse, galley (kitchen), head (bathroom), and cabins (living quarters). The rest of the area in the hull and superstructure will be filled with fuel tanks, ballast tanks, water tanks, and various storage compartments. Since tugboats are working

The *Ervin S. Cooper* is a perfect example of a working-class tug. While many new tugboats ply the waters, the vast majority of America's tugboats are older boats such as the *Cooper*. This is not because tugboat companies are cheap and won't buy new boats. It's just that tugboats are so tough they last a long, long time.

Any tour must begin with the pilothouse. It is the highest part of the hull and the command center of the boat. This is where the captain spends most of his working life. It affords views all around so the captain can keep an eye on all that is going on around his boat.

boats, their deck layout and the positioning of towing equipment are generally mandated by the physics of the type of job the tugboat will perform. How and where this equipment is placed is critical and must be precisely engineered. And while much effort is made to maximize performance when designing a tugboat, the designer must also remember that the tugboat will also become a *home* for the crew. A good tugboat allows crew members to be comfortable when off duty so that they will be fresh and well rested on duty. The design must also allow for some privacy and elbowroom. When human beings are enclosed in a small space for an extended period of time, small annoyances can become large annoyances. If a crew is at each others' throats, performance will drop and accidents are more likely to occur. The importance of "livability" cannot be overstressed when discussing tugboat design.

The tugboats shown in this chapter are owned and operated by Crescent Towing, which has had over 50 years of experience in the ports of the Southeast. Crescent Towing currently operates 25 tugboats dispersed between the ports of Mobile, Alabama (its headquarters); New Orleans, Louisiana; and Savannah, Georgia. Its mix of tugboats illustrates the variety of tugs used throughout the nation. The newest boat in the fleet is the year-old, ultramodern, 5,000-horsepower tractor tug *Point Clear*, currently operating in New Orleans. The age and power of the rest of its boats varies widely. Many of the boats are older hulls that have been completely refitted with modern engines, reduction gears, propellers, Kort nozzles, and towing gear.

In terms of tonnage, the port of Mobile is the nation's 14th-largest port, and it is a tricky port in which to operate a tug. The channels are narrow, with little margin for error. The turning basin, where tugs turn the ships around, is quite small. The port requires pinpoint control, which often necessitates very

The pilothouse features controls on both the port and starboard sides. These dual controls allow the captain to work from either side of the boat, always allowing him the best visibility. Standard controls include throttle controls (one for each engine), engine gauges, three or four radios, GPS, and a radio. The steering wheel has been replaced with a single steering rod. While nowhere near as beautiful, this method of steering has its advantages. The position or angle of the rod is the same as the position or angle of the rudder. This allows the captain to know exactly where the rudder is at all times, a task that is difficult with a conventional wheel.

All piping and wiring in the engine room, and all over the boat, is kept very clean so that any leaks will be visible, and all are labeled so the crew can see exactly what is leaking.

short towlines and awkward tug positioning. Crescent Towing's Mobile fleet has three fine examples of working harbor tugs: the *Ervin S. Cooper*, the *Alabama*, and the *Mardi Gras*. Each of these boats performs roughly the same duties, primarily ship docking and sailing. While they look very similar, each has unique features. The *Ervin S. Cooper* is a twin-engine, single-screw boat. She is 107 feet LOA (length overall), has a beam (width) of 26 feet, and draws (the distance from the waterline to the deepest part of the hull) 11 feet. The boat was originally used as the New York Harbor fireboat. When it was retired from service, Crescent Towing purchased it. She was stripped and refitted with a new superstructure and all of the gear necessary to turn her into a tugboat. This included the winches, bitts, heavier fenders, and a reinforced bow.

The *Alabama* is also a twin-engine boat, but with twin screws and rated at 3,500 total horsepower. At only 85 feet in length, she is the smallest tugboat in Crescent's Mobile fleet. The *Alabama* is 24 feet across the beam and draws 9.3 feet of water.

The *Mardi Gras* is a tugboat that just keeps on tugging. She has a single engine and single screw. She is usually the third boat in the batting order when a call comes in, but she still sees a lot of work. The *Mardi Gras* is 103 feet LOA, has a beam of 25 feet, and draws 11.6 feet. Her single 251 ALCO engine produces around 3,000 horsepower and drives a single 108-inch-diameter propeller.

The heart of a tug is her engine room. It is the largest room in the tug and houses engines, generators, pumps, and all of the wiring, piping, and equipment to support them.

A walk through the engine room, the galley, the head, the cabins, the pilothouse, and the deck of these three boats will show layouts typical of all tugboats throughout the nation.

The Engine Room

The heart of any tugboat is the engine, or in the case of many modern tugs, the engines. The tugboat's engine power, combined with the reduction gear and propellers, provides the muscle that allows a 100-foot-long tug to pull a 900-foot-long freighter. To do this, a tug captain needs power, and as a result, the largest internal space on a harbor tugboat is the engine room.

Tugboats use a wide variety of diesel engines, with 10-, 12-, and 16-cylinder models most common. They may be turbocharged or not and, depending on size, can be rated from 1,200 total horsepower for single-engine craft to over 20,000 horsepower for multiple-engine monsters.

The tugs *Alabama* and *Ervin S. Cooper* both have a very traditional layout. Twin diesel engines transmit power through twin reduction gears. The *Mardi Gras*, an older boat, has the classic single engine driving a single propeller.

The engines on the *Ervin S. Cooper*, two 567C EMD 12-cylinder diesels, are typical for

Most harbor tugboat engines have 16 cylinders or more and produce as much as 3,000 horsepower.

a twin-engine harbor tug. The EMDs are General Motors power plants, and these produce about 2,100 horsepower each, giving the captain 4,200 total horsepower. The 567 number in the engine's name refers to the cubic inches per cylinder. That makes for a total of 6,804 cubic inches per engine. The cylinders are arranged in a V-12 arrangement, with the cylinders on a 45 degree angle. Other statistics of interest concerning the engines are just as impressive. Each engine weighs 25,596 pounds. Each piston weighs 42 pounds, and the crankshaft alone weighs 7,851 pounds. They have a 9 1/16-inch bore with a 10-inch stroke. Each engine holds more than 100 gallons of oil, and its oil pump supplies at a rate of 105 gallons per minute at 900 rpm at 40–70 psi.

To power these engines, the *Ervin S. Cooper* has four fuel tanks with a total capacity of 27,000 gallons. At 750 rpm, the engine burns around 1.5 gallons per minute. At 900 rpm this increases to 1.8 gallons per minute.

One big advantage of the EMD engines is the fact that the blocks are made of steel, unlike many made of cast iron. This allows the blocks to be weld-repaired with a high degree of confidence in the event of damage, thus allowing for longer engine life.

Engines are mounted on thick and strong reinforced frames. A great deal of torque is generated on the mounts when the engine is at maximum throttle, so they must be strong. Breaking a motor mount in a car can be a problem, but doing the same with a 25,000-pound diesel engine can be catastrophic.

The *Alabama*'s engines are two 3512 Caterpillar 12-cylinder diesels, which combine to produce around 3,500 horsepower. The *Mardi Gras*, on the other hand, must get by with its

single engine, a 3,000-horsepower, 12-cylinder, 251 ALCO diesel.

Full engine controls, like the ones the captain has in the pilothouse, are also located in the engine room. If the control systems in the pilothouse fail, the captain can still control the engines by giving radio commands to the engineer in the engine room.

The reduction gear is bolted up to the rear of the engine. This reduces the rpm from the engine to the propeller shaft. Reduction gears usually range from 5 to 1 to 3 to 1, depending on the boat, engine type and speed, and propeller combination. A 3 to 1 reduction gear will

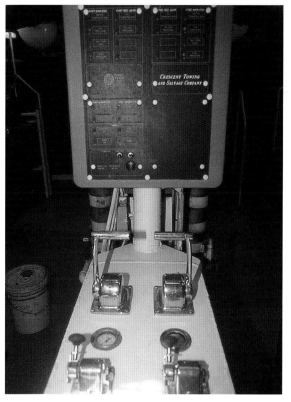

(above, right) A complete set of engine controls, just like the ones the captain uses in the pilothouse, are located in the engine room. If the controls in the pilothouse fail, the engineer can control the engines from the engine room, taking radio commands from the captain.

Because of the large volume of oil used in their large diesel engines and the importance of keeping the oil clean, tugboats have very large oil filtering systems. While expensive, their cost is offset by longer engine life.

take an engine running at 900 rpm and drop the propeller speed to 300 rpm. Tugboats are geared to produce more torque and less speed than boats of equal size that operate at higher top speeds. A tug makes power by slowly turning a large propeller instead of turning a smaller prop more rapidly. From the reduction gear, the propeller shafts runs under the deck and through the hull to the propellers.

The propellers on a tugboat must be big and sit deep in the water. Just like in drag racing, power is useless unless it can be "hooked up." Therefore, tugboat propellers are large in proportion to the overall size of the craft. A 100-foot tug will have much more prop than a 100-foot yacht. The *Ervin S. Cooper* has one four-blade, 79-inch prop surrounded by a Kort nozzle. The *Alabama* has two five-blade, 69-inch-diameter props, and the *Mardi Gras* has one five-blade, 108-inch-diameter propeller.

Not only does the tugboat's engine room house the engines, it also contains the tugboat's generators. These provide power for all of the boat's electrical systems. A single generator on the *Alabama* has an output of 75 kilowatts (75,000 watts—enough to power 750 100-watt lightbulbs). By utilizing generators, the tugboats can run AC electrical systems,

Water that is used to cool the engines is brought in through the hull, circulated around the engines, and then pumped back out.

which are less expensive than DC systems, and thus eliminate all of the headaches of batteries. One generator is running at all times, while the other is a backup. This also allows maintenance to be done on the generators without the tugboat losing electrical power, or if one generator fails, the tug can still operate.

Air compressors are also located in the engine room. Constant air supply is needed because many of the boat's controls are pneumatic. These include most of the captain's pilothouse controls, such as the throttles and clutches. The engine room also houses both the hydraulic pumps for the boat's rudder system and water pumps for the fire fighting systems. While holding a great deal of the boat's mechanical systems, the engine rooms are still relatively roomy to allow for easy maintenance and repairs.

A large diesel generator supplies electricity throughout the boat. Although one such generator will supply enough power for the tugboat, most boats have two. A backup allows maintenance to be performed without interfering with the tug's operation, and in the rare case of a generator failure there will be a backup, which can be brought on-line quickly.

To most of the crew, this is the most important part of the boat. In between jobs, some mean meals are cooked here. The galley includes all of the conveniences of home, including oven, stove, refrigerator, and microwave.

One other use of the engine room is to restore body heat. Tugboat crews must often work in cold and wet conditions, and on occasion tug crews will rescue people from the water. In such instances, the heat of the engine room will provide the quickest way to restore body heat. Unfortunately, a hot engine room also means misery for the engineer during the warm summer months.

Living Quarters

On all three of Crescent Towing's boats, each crew member has private quarters, also known as cabins. The captain's quarters are located closest to the pilothouse. This position allows him the shortest path from his berth to the tugboat's controls. The engineer gets the loudest and usually hottest quarters (again,

bad in summer, good in winter), located to the rear of the boat near the engine room. This position allows the engineer to get from his berth to his workstation as fast as possible. The two deck hands' berths are in separate cabins just off of the galley.

While the accommodations are not luxurious, they are roomy (for boat standards) and comfortable. The crews work seven days on and seven days off. While on watch, they stay on the boat. Ships often sail and make port during the night and early morning, so the boat must be ready 24 hours a day. As a result, captain and crew must grab sleep when they can, which is often between jobs during the day. A private, comfortable bed is a must if each crew member is to remain effective during the entire watch.

The Galley

Whether it is a weeklong barge push or a watch for a harbor tug, the crew stays on the boat. When not under way, the center of activity is the galley. It is the social center for the boat. Not only do the crew members eat here; they also watch television, play cards and, most of all, tell stories during the delays in between jobs. It is here that the captain reviews jobs with the crew, congratulating them when all goes well, or retraining them when something goes wrong. The crews eat well, and the food is good. When on a watch of seven straight days and nights, members of the crew don't see their families, and their activities are limited to things that can be done on the boat. As a result, meals become a major event, which each crew member looks forward to. Cooking and eating become one of the greatest pleasures on the boat. Tugboat work is often moments of intense activity followed by hours of inactivity, and since the crew is often working on a job during traditional meal hours, it provides them with the excuse to cook pretty much all of the time.

Since the tug runs on an alternating current, standard appliances can be used. The galley is well equipped with a large stove/oven, refrigerator/freezer, microwave, and double sink. Wood cabinets provide a place for storage while adding a comfortable feel to the galley. Due to the sheer of the hull, the floor of the galley is not flat, but angles down from bow to stern. As a result, it is a walk uphill from the sink to the table and downhill from the table to the sink.

The Pilothouse

If the engine room is the heart of the tugboat, the pilothouse is the brain. It is from the

Toughness is the first, second, and third requirement of a tugboat hull. A tugboat will be in thousands of controlled collisions throughout its life, and probably a few uncontrolled ones. Regardless of the other features of the hull, if it is not tough, it will not last.

pilothouse (and occasionally the doghouse) that the captain runs the boat. The pilothouse is located on the highest of the boat's three levels.

A good field of view is critical. The tugboat captain must be able to see all that is going on around him. Modern tugboat pilothouses closely resemble control towers at airports. Not only must the captain have a 360 degree

While the *Ervin S. Cooper* is in dry dock, a better view of the hull contours is possible. An older boat, her hull is made of rolled steel, welded together on steel frames. Often the bow of the tug is the strongest area of the hull. After all, it is where the pushing will be done. During a refit, the *Ervin S. Cooper* gets some pieces of angled steel to reinforce the bow.

field of view, but he must also be able to look up at the ship he is working with and down on the deck to watch the crew handling the lines.

Like any other part of the tug, the pilot-house must be tough. Many ships have sides that overhang, and it is only a matter of time before the house is damaged. In order to lessen this likelihood, some boats have "training wheels" fixed to each side of the house. These take the brunt of any collision between the house and ship, and allow the tugboat to "ride" up and down against the side of the ship without damaging either vessel.

Over the past 20 years, the tugboats' controls and electronic equipment have changed dramatically. The classic steering wheel has been replaced by levers and dials. In the case of the *Alabama*, a lever is used. Its position relative to the centerline of the boat is the same as the rudders. This allows the captain to quickly know the position of the rudder and also allows him to quickly put the rudder into the position that he wants. While steering levers are nowhere as lovely at the old wood and brass spoke wheels, they are more efficient. Throttles are controlled with two levers located to the side of the steering lever. Each engine has its own throttle, which allows it to be operated independently. When the lever is pushed all the way forward, the engine is all "ahead full." When it is pulled all the way back, it is in "full back." When the lever is

The ability to steer in tight space is largely due to the large rudders located behind large propellers that are surrounded by Kort nozzles. Note the zinc anode built up on this ship. The propeller shaft runs from the reduction gear, through the hull, to the propeller. These shafts are solid steel, a necessity to handle the torque of the engine and the resistance of the propeller.

straight up in the center, it is in a neutral or "clutch" position.

There are two sets of controls in the pilothouse, one located on the starboard side and the other on the port side. This allows the captain to work either side of the boat, depending on which side he is pushing. Various gauges give the status of the craft to the captain. Common equipment includes a compass, engine tachometer, shaft speed indicator, depth sounders, Global Positioning System, and radar.

The pilothouse includes a number of radios for the captain's communication needs. In the case of the *Alabama* it is four marine radios. This allows the captain to have one radio on channel 16 (the common communication channel); one radio on a channel chosen for the tugboat, ship captain, and pilot during a docking job; and one radio with which to communicate with company headquarters. The forth radio in the pilothouse is a hand-held one, so that the captain can still communicate in case he has to move around the boat. These radios have additional speakers and microphones in the galley and cabins, allowing for quick responses if the crew happens to be below.

The electronic equipment carried on tugboats has changed greatly over the last 30 years, especially in navigation assistance. Tugboat captains now have use of reasonably powerful radar systems. With a range that can be changed from as close as one-quarter of a mile

The bullnose is used when running a line from the bow of the boat. Its centerline location assures that the tension on the line will be loaded on the center of the boat.

(GPS). These systems triangulate from signals received from satellites, giving a captain his location within a few feet anywhere in the world. In fog and foul weather, the GPS can keep a captain in the channel or allow him to find particular markers when visibility is measured in the tens of feet. Locations can also be stored in the GPS, allowing the captain to chart underwater obstacles and other hazards. Simply put, GPS can make the difference between being lost or knowing exactly where you are.

However, there is a danger associated with all of these new electronic systems. While they are relatively cheap, very accurate, pretty simple to use, and allow for much safer voyages, a captain must still know how to navigate his craft without them. When they break—and things usually break at the worst time—the captain must still get his crew and cargo safely home. It must also be remembered that information is no good if it is not used. All of this equipment and more was on the Exxon *Valdez*, and her crew still drove her onto a rock.

The Deck

The deck of the tugboat is thoughtfully and strategically laid out. The positioning of certain equipment is done for reasons gained through experience and an understanding of the physics associated with moving ships. The "bullnose" is located high and as far forward on the bow as possible without the danger of coming into contact with the ship's side when assisting. The bullnose controls the headlines and spring lines run from the bow of the tugboat to the ship being assisted. The aperture of the bullnose must be large enough for very large ropes to pass through. These ropes are commonly 6 inches or more in diameter.

all the way out to 46 miles, it allows the captain to see approaching weather, other watercraft, and navigation markers when visibility is poor.

A highly accurate electronic depth sounder keeps the captain informed of depth at all times. This is important when bringing a ship with a 45-foot draft up a 50-foot-deep channel. It also allows the captain to pick up a change in the depth of the channel, even when he is not assisting a ship. This knowledge may come in handy when assisting a ship or may initiate dredging operations.

Another relatively new addition to the maritime fleet is the Global Positioning System

The deck of a tug is strategically designed. The location of the main fixtures, guides, and bitts is determined by where the best physical advantage and stability will be gained. The steel grid at the rear of the deck covers the rudder's control rods. These grids can be removed so that the equipment can be easily maintained and repaired. Large H bitts are used to secure lines when working a job. The wear marks on these steel fixtures attest to the tremendous pressures associated with moving ships.

After the rope is passed through the bullnose, it is secured to an H bitt, a massive cleat used to secure the towline. Smaller H bitts may be located along the sides of the tug, and another large H bitt is located on the rear deck. (The rear bitt is used when the tugboat is pulling.) The positioning of these bitts is very important. In order for the tugboat to be able to maneuver well, the location of the H bitt relative to the rudders and propellers is critical and will have a tremendous impact on how the tug reacts under load. Usually the best location for the rear bitt is about one-third of the tugboat's length from the stern.

Towing or "pelican" hooks are used on many tugs. Like the rear H bitt, the pelican hook is used for pulling. However, they have one great advantage over H-bitts: they can be quickly released, whereas a line tied to an H bitt must be untied or cut. There are three pneumatic release switches (one in the pilothouse, one in the doghouse, and one on the rear deck) and two mechanical releases on the hook itself. The pelican hook is located in the same area as the stern H bitt for maximum handling ability. It is built on a swivel so that the line does not have to chaff when going side to side.

The rear deck of the boat may also have a large winch, used to bring in line when towing.

Large cleats are located on the rear deck for securing various lines when towing. The rudder control equipment is exposed above the deck on most tugs. This allows for easier maintenance and repairs. The system is covered by fitted steel grating, allowing the crew to work around this equipment without danger.

The Hull

Perhaps the primary reason that tugboats last as long as they do is the fact that they are heavily overbuilt. When a tugboat is designed, the builders know that the boat will be involved in countless controlled collisions and most likely a few uncontrolled ones as well. The boat must be incredibly tough, so they build it incredibly tough, and then add a little more strength just to make sure. This toughness starts with hull design. When a tug is seen working on the water, most of the hull is invisible. Tugboats draw much more water than people think. This is to get the tug's big propellers deep in the water.

Tugboats have a pure displacement hull. That means that they "push" the water aside in order to move. On the other hand, planing and semiplaning hulls "ride" on the water to some degree at speed. As a result, displacement hulls are much slower than planing hulls, but are much more stable.

The classic harbor and oceangoing tugboats usually have a fairly narrow hull design. This design provides for low resistance when pushing a ship. The hulls are built of steel and are heavily reinforced, especially in the bow, stern, and around all of the areas where towlines

While the steel hull of a tugboat is tough, it still needs protection. Used aircraft tires are chained to the side of the hull to absorb impacts, and large rollers are welded to the side of the house to protect it as it rides up and down the side of the tug. Without these rollers, both the ship's hull and the tug's house would be damaged.

will be secured, such as the H bitts and deck fittings. In the rear of the boat the freeboard is low. The sides of the rear of the hull are tumbled home, meaning that instead of flaring up and out, the sides curve up and in. This keeps the top of the side of the tugboat from making contact with the side of a ship.

Tugboat hull construction has changed over the years, and many of the so-called technological advances in construction technique have had an interesting side effect: they have kept older hulls in operation. While newly built hulls are good, solid hulls, they are constructed in a different manner than the older ones. And many in the tugboat industry like the old way. Older tugboat hulls are most likely constructed of thick plate steel, rolled to form the curves of the hull. Modern hulls are often flat-plate steel, cut into precise geometric plates and then welded together. The turn of the hull on these boats is not a smooth arc, but more like the facets of a jewel. While the hulls look curved, they are actually flat pieces with angled joints. The reason for this change in construction technique is primarily cost. As one tugboat man put it, "The difference between old hulls and new hulls is like the difference in kicking a 1953 Buick and kicking a 1995 Honda. You put a big dent in the Honda, and the Buick breaks your foot." This devotion to older hulls is one of the reasons that many tugboat companies refit older hulls with modern equipment.

Regardless of type and age, the outer hull is blanketed with fenders to avoid damage to the hull while assisting a ship. Fenders come in many forms. Most tugboats have thick, solid rubber strips bolted all along the hull, especially in the bow and stern—areas sure to be in contact with ships. While these help, they are not enough. The outer layer of defense is made up of large tires (usually worn-out tractor or aircraft tires) chained to the sides. These recycled fenders are the most effective in the business. They are cheap, plentiful, and give the tugboats much of their working-man image. Perhaps the most aesthetically pleasing fenders are the bow fenders made up from old towline, cut into pieces, and laid over the bow, giving the tug a "woolly," friendly look.

CHAPTER FOUR

Tugboat Crews

The tug captains and crews live a mostly solitary existence, slowly plying their trade in the rivers, harbors, and oceans of the world. Incredible loads, loads that would pack our interstates and rail lines, are silently and slowly transported across the waterways almost without notice. Even though tugging is a slow process, the crews have little time to relax. Their days and nights are full of work and watches. They battle current, wind, narrow channels, other watercraft, bad weather, and every other oddity that rivers, ports, and oceans can throw at a captain and crew. They must also battle monotony, which causes lack of attention; and lack of attention is one of the greatest dangers on the water. Every job on a

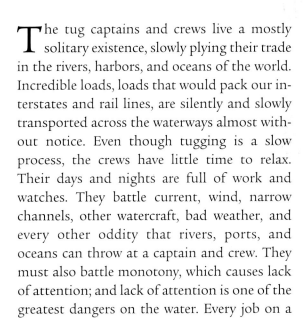

If you have to work, this is not a bad place to do it. The captain not only runs the boats controls; he is responsible for all of the actions of his crew, their training, and the boat's condition, as well as all regulatory compliance.

67

During a single day, a tugboat captain has many different views from his office window. They range from the tranquillity of a beautiful sunset and the blindness of rain and fog to the sight of a huge tanker crashing against the side of the tug.

tug is important and must be done properly and safely. It is the captain's job to see that this is done.

Captain

On any tugboat or ship, the buck stops with the captain. He is responsible for all that goes on aboard his tug, including all actions of his crew and all of the maneuvers that his tugboat makes. When under way, the captain's primary hands-on job is driving the boat. When on a job, a harbor tug captain communicates commands with either the ship's captain or the local pilot. They radio to the tug captain the speed and direction in which they want the tug to work, and the tug captain makes the appropriate adjustments to throttle and rudder. On occasion the tug captain may offer advice, but most often he responds without question. This is especially true when a captain is working with a pilot he is familiar with and trusts.

Tugboating has often been referred to as a family business. It is not uncommon to see fathers, sons, and brothers captaining tugs in the same port. Many a captain's son grew up around the boats. Their first job was often on either

The engineer's job is to keep the boat in shape. This includes both routine and nonroutine tasks, from the everyday chores of checking the fuel and oil levels to large projects such as engine rebuilds and hull repainting. Here a boat's engineer checks the fuel level of the craft. Not trusting this job to gauges, he checks the level with long, metal dipsticks. The engineer's life is made up of routine. A good engineer will find a way to keep an eye on every piece of the boat. Some parts of the boat are checked daily, others at less frequent intervals.

Occasionally tugboats must come out of the water. The reason can be anything from a propeller repair to a total hull cleaning. It is only when the tugboat is out of the water that repairs below the waterline can be made.

their father's boat or one in the company's fleet. As a result, many families have three and four generations that have worked on tugboats. Very often tugboat captains truly began their training as young children. The stories, advice, and exposure given by their fathers slowly sank in. As young boys they most likely could con a small boat better than their peers, and did so observing the rules and courtesies of the water (facts which have escaped the vast majority of today's jet-skiing idiots). They understood navigation better than other boys their age and most likely tied the best (and most complicated) knots. This lifetime training they received growing up and the respect and pride that they have for their profession are some of the reasons that today's tugboat captains are among the safest machine operators in the country.

Before and after. Engine cooling is accomplished by using seawater instead of a closed radiator system like a car. The water is taken in through ports in the hull. These photos of the same port before and after cleaning show the intense effect seawater has on boats.

The road to captaincy usually begins as deck hand. Most captains came up through the ranks, serving duty as both deck hand and engineer before assuming the position of captain. Their careers as master seamen begin with the most basic tasks. As a deck hand they learn the way lines are handled, the layout of the boat, how the equipment operates, and how it is serviced. They also observe the way their captain handles the boat. They gain experience, and if they show aptitude their next job will be that of boat engineer. It is in this job that the future captain really learns the boat. Engineers are the guys who get called when something breaks, and it greatly disappoints everyone involved if he cannot fix it. He is also the guy who gets in trouble if the boat does not meet one of its various inspections. If an engineer masters his job and shows the proper aptitude, he may have an opportunity to try for captain. A good tugboat captain will begin to allow a candidate to run the helm when it is safe to do so. The candidate will spend more time in the pilothouse receiving training from the captain. During this time the candidate will also study. And study. Practical experience is invaluable to a captain, but to become a captain the candidate must first be qualified by the Coast Guard. It is required that each candidate for captain must first have 1,080 days of documented sea time on a vessel. Once this time has been accumulated the candidate must pass the Coast Guard's 200-ton, 200-mile certification. This test covers rules of the road, plotting and navigation, fire fighting, and proper ways to do deck work. Once licensed, the captains can command any tugboat with a displacement of 200 tons or less (which includes most of them) and can operate their craft up to 200 miles from shore. This certification process is repeated every five years.

Once he has passed the tests, the candidate becomes a captain. When a new captain takes his first command, he will often work for a while with another, more experienced captain in the pilothouse. This helps a new captain through a very difficult stage. As deck hand and engineer, the new captain never had the ultimate authority. He always had someone to fall back on—the captain. Now he is the one who everyone else has to be able to fall back on. Even if a new captain has been on tugs for many years, when he becomes the ultimate authority on his boat and is solely responsible for the actions of his boat and crew, things become very tense for him.

Deck Hand

The deck hand's primary job is to work the lines of the tugboat. Whether bringing a distressed ship into port or helping a loaded freighter get out to sea, the deck hands work the lines. This can be dangerous work. In adverse conditions the normally simple job of passing a line to the ship may become nearly impossible. In rough seas harbor tugs can generate a great deal of pitch and roll. Waves crash over the bow. And most jobs require two hands, making holding on difficult. Add to this 40- to 50-knot winds, air temperatures in the teens, and water temperatures in the 40s, and things quickly become miserable.

Lines are still passed the way they have been for centuries. The tug captain matches speed with the ship and brings the tugboat close alongside. The deck hand, with the help of a "monkey fist" knot, throws the line to the crew of the ship. This light nylon line is tied to the towline and is used to hoist the towline aboard the ship. It is looped on the end, and this loop is passed around a cleat on the ship. If the tugboat is going to pull the ship with the bow, the line is passed through the bullnose and made fast to the H bitt. If the tug is to tow from the stern, the line is attached to the pelican hook located on the rear deck. This hook allows for 180 degrees of swivel and has three separate quick-release systems in case the boat gets into trouble while towing.

When not working a job, the deck hands help the boat's engineer keep the boat and the lines in proper working condition. This is a full-time job, especially in saltwater environments. Day in and day out, the most common job is painting. Tugboats are made of steel and they continually rust. Chipping old paint and

Repairing large components such as a propeller shaft is a complex and costly job. Few parts in a tug's propulsion system can be moved easily.

applying new is a full-time proposition. With the crew constantly touching up the paint job, the whole boat above the waterline is repainted about every year.

Inspecting and repairing towlines also falls to the deck hands. Lines absorb a great deal of stress and are often "pinched" between the ship and the bow of the tug. If heavy damage occurs, the line must be cut and spliced. This is a critical job. If a line breaks during tow it is extremely dangerous to the crew and will disconnect the ship from the tug, meaning a loss of control.

In addition to all of the regular hazards of the sea, broken lines are extremely dangerous to the deck hands. As one deck hand remarked, "Once the line is secure I go back inside. I don't go back out until the captain tells me to release the line." A healthy respect for towlines can keep a deck hand alive. New synthetic lines now on the market have made things safer (not safe, but safer). They have very little stretch, and as a result, when they break they normally just fall straight down. Older polypropylene lines had more stretch and as a result when they broke they came straight back across the

This propeller is secured to the shaft with one large nut, and to tighten a nut this big you need a big wrench. Note the chain attached to the wrench to allow the necessary torque to tighten it and another attached to the propeller to keep it from spinning.

deck like a whip. The most dangerous towing line is wire. Large 1- to 2-inch cable is still often used to pull ships. If they break, not only do they come across the deck like a steel whip; they also uncoil at the same time, making it impossible to gauge in which direction they will go. The most terrible stories heard on the tugs are those of deck hands being literally cut in two by broken wire cables.

Engineer

The engineer's job is to keep the tug in top running condition. If something goes wrong or breaks, it will be the engineer's job to make repairs. However, the goal of all engineers is to keep the boat in such shape as to make break-downs very unlikely. This is done through preventative maintenance. The engineer may call on the rest of the crew to assist in maintenance, but it is the *responsibility* of the engineer. The engineer's job may range from overseeing the installation of new engines to daily checks of the boat's fuel, water, and oil status.

Most of the engineer's time is spent in the engine room, and there is plenty of equipment there to keep him busy. The 85-foot *Alabama* is a perfect example. While it is the smallest harbor tug in Crescent Towing's Mobile fleet, the *Alabama* still poses a maintenance challenge. The engineer must deal with two V-12 Caterpillar diesel engines, two reduction gears, two generators, two compressors, a 50,000-ton winch with its own engine, oil recovery and filtering systems, and engine cooling systems that pick up seawater for cooling purposes. Add to this all of the electronics, hundreds of feet of wiring and piping, controls, valves, and hundreds of other pieces of support equipment, and you start to get the picture of the headaches an engineer faces. Keep in mind that all of this equipment is housed in a structure that moves up and down, side to side, front to back, and, to top it all off, makes a living running into things.

The boat's engineer does have help in the form of the port engineer, who works for the tugboat company and oversees all of the maintenance on all of the tugboats in a particular port. Usually all of a company's boats are different in terms of engine size, layout, and control systems. Whenever possible, equipment such as compressors and generators is standardized, making maintenance easier.

As mentioned before, the most routine, day-to-day maintenance task is chipping and painting. From tugboat deck hands to naval personnel, all saltwater seamen know the routine—sailors spend their lives saving boats, while saltwater spends its life killing them . . . and the saltwater always wins. It is corrosive to most metals and to *all* of the affordable ones. From a distance, ships that have been recently painted look smooth, shiny, and clean. Up close they are only shiny and clean. The texture of the side of the ship is rolling with the worn faces of previous paint jobs.

Engine maintenance is also done on a routine basis. Just like your family car's engine, the oil and filter need changing. However, with these engines, the oil capacity is 110 quarts, while the family car only requires 4 1/2 quarts. As a result, the oil filters in tugboats are massive and do a much better job of filtering than an automotive filter, allowing for longer oil life.

Engine diagnostic work is done in various ways. Vibration analysis can show wear in bearings and pumps. One of the more interesting methods of measuring engine performance is oil analysis. Oil samples taken from an engine are analyzed for metal content. Depending on the levels of particular metals present, the engineer will know where to look for a problem. For example, the main engine (crankshaft) bearings are surfaced in silver. If the analysis shows an abnormally high level of silver, the engineer will know he has a wear problem on his main bearings.

Pilots

It is not possible to properly describe the work of the tugboats without a word on pilots. Pilots are local seamen who assist the ship captains and tugboat captains getting the ships into and out of port. Major ports throughout the world have pilots, and they are often former tugboat captains.

The deck hands' job is to work the deck (no big surprise there). They handle lines when the tug is assisting a ship. A complete understanding of lines and securing methods is a must. However, mere knowledge is not enough. A deck hand must have a complete respect for the forces that are present when working lines. If a line—or even worse, a steel cable—breaks when under load, it will snap back like a large whip. It can kill a deck hand in the blink of an eye, and it will give very little warning when it goes.

While not on a job, the deck hands help maintain the boat, and that usually means painting. The sea seems to have a particular dislike for anything metal and spends a good bit of its time trying to kill it.

Where the pilot boards the ship varies from port to port. It primarily depends on the obstructions that the ship will encounter upon entering port. In some ports the ships may come in very close on their own and may only need piloting for a mile or so. More hazardous ports, with narrow channels, strong currents, or other obstructions, may require a pilot to be on board for many miles. Regardless of distance, the pilot's knowledge of the local waters will far exceed that of the ship's captain, who may be coming into a port for the first time. Many captains constantly visit foreign ports where differences in language and navigation markers make navigating very confusing. And while maritime charts have become both more plentiful and more accurate, the bottom of the sea constantly changes. An obstruction may have formed by the time a new chart is being printed. It is impossible for any ship's captain to know all of the ports of the world as well as the local pilots do.

When a ship is coming into a port it radios for the pilot. The pilot is taken out to the ship on the port's pilot boat. Pilot boats are tough little boats. They are very seaworthy, as they must often work in very rough weather.

Getting aboard the ship can often be a frightening experience for the pilot. The normal method is for the pilot boat to match speed with the ship and to come close alongside. The pilot, while standing on the deck of the pilot boat, must grab a Jacob's ladder and then climb it up the side of the ship. This can be tricky and dangerous, especially in rough weather. The ladders are made of rope and are difficult to climb in the best of conditions. The crew of the tugboat *Alabama* can attest to this. On December 29, 1995, a local pilot was boarding a freighter in rough weather. A problem with the ladder resulted in the pilot falling about 35 feet and landing on the hard metal deck of the pilot boat. The crews of the *Alabama* and the pilot boat fashioned a makeshift stretcher from the tugboat's galley door and transported the badly injured pilot to the *Alabama*'s engine room to try to prevent hypothermia. From there, the tugboat abandoned the freighter in the channel and quickly transported the pilot to an oil rig in the area. It was the quickest way to get the pilot medical care. From the oil rig the pilot was airlifted to a hospital in the rig's helicopter. While the pilot was badly injured, he did survive the incident.

This is an example not only of the dangers that pilots face, but also of the many roles that tugboat crews must be prepared for when venturing to sea. It is one of the oldest traditions of the sea that thoughts of self are turned away when someone else is in trouble on the water.

Once aboard the ship, the pilot pretty much takes over from the captain. While the captain is still in command, he will most likely defer speed and course commands to the pilot. When the pilot has brought the ship into the port and to the proper dock, the ship, with the help of the tugboats, will commence docking. In some ports the piloting of the docking of the ship is treated as a separate job. In this case a "docking pilot" will take over from the pilot who brought the ship into port.

When the docking begins, many pilots begin to show their tugboat roots. Many pilots are ex-tugboat captains, and it is generally recognized in the industry that they make the best pilots. After all, it is logical that a pilot who has run tugboats will better understand their capabilities. During a docking the pilot becomes the orchestra conductor. Often more than one tug is used to dock a ship. It is the pilot's task to combine the power of the tugboat's engines, the ship's engines, and the control of all of their rudders to dock with the minimum of effort. The pilot may also have at his command bow thrusters on both tugboat and ship. He also will try to use the wind and current when maneuvering a ship. When allowed to do their job, pilots save ports and shipping companies a great deal of money. Likewise, failure to respect a pilot's opinion can cost a captain. Even slow impacts are hazardous to large ships. One freighter captain coming out of Mobile learned this lesson the hard way. He overrode the pilot's command while turning around in port, bounced his rudder off of a dock, and had a $7 million repair bill.

CHAPTER FIVE

Maneuvering a Tugboat

The national fleet of more than 6,000 tug-boats and pushboats and 31,000 barges has a combined carrying capacity of over 89 million tons (the number of boats and barges registered with the American Waterways Operators). The tugboat industry employs more than 30,000 people, and each year the fleet moves almost 800 million tons of raw materials and finished goods. This accounts for around 15 percent of all of the freight moved in the United States.

While it may appear that a tugboat casually motors up and pushes against the side of a ship, it is far more complex. Both the power applied and the position on the ship are carefully chosen. Power must be carefully controlled, and the position the tug takes on the ship determines how much leverage the tug will have.

When assisting a ship, the bow is usually the business end of the tug. Tremendous pressures are applied, and while the hull and "factory" fenders are probably enough to handle the load, a little insurance (here in the form of a Goodyear tractor tire) never hurts. *Mack Burt*

The beauty of the tugboat fleet is that it allows the United States to take advantage of one of its greatest natural resources—the nation's 25,000-mile waterway system. While 15 percent of the nation's freight is moved by tugboats every year, the tugboat industry accounts for only 2 percent of the amount spent yearly on shipping in America. And if you stand beside a tugboat captain, whether he is bringing a 1,000-foot barge assembly through a narrow bridge opening or putting a 900-foot freighter into a crowded dock, he makes it look easy. A tugboat captain makes corrections in wheel and throttle and handles these huge loads seemingly as easy as driving a car down the road. But let him hand you the controls and it gets very tough, very fast. It is the captain's years of experience that allows him to comfortably handle situations in which one wrong command can mean disaster.

A tugboat captain is constantly feeling and sensing many things and is processing all of the information in his head. As discussed in chapter 4, the reason for this is the knowledge and experience gained throughout his career. While his maneuvers look casual, they are actually carefully and precisely calculated before they begin.

The pilot and captain use standard boat-handling techniques that are based on basic principles of physics. The techniques used in ship and barge handling are a function of both force and leverage. The force side of the equation is pretty obvious. A tugboat has big engines and big propellers; thus, it can provide lots of force. However, captains and pilots more often rely on leverage. The less power expended by the ship and tug executing a maneuver, the better. But before captains and pilots can apply these maneuvers to a job, they must understand three things: the handling characteristics of their own tugboat, the handling of the ship being worked, and how the elements (wind and current) will affect the job.

A tugboat captain must first understand all of the handling characteristics of his own tugboat. Many factors can influence the way a tug handles, such as the type of hull, engine, and propulsion system. But there are also other variables that will influence a tugboat's performance. For instance, a tugboat with full water and fuel tanks will handle differently than it will when the tanks are closer to empty. With full tanks it will ride lower in the water and will not be as affected by wind, but will be more affected by current. A craft with full tanks will also be slower to respond to engine commands. Not only does total weight matter to a tugboat, but where it is located is also important. Fuel and water tanks are often located along most of the length of the hull. As tanks begin to empty, the trim of the boat may change. If the boat becomes heavy in the bow and light in the stern, the propeller may lose its bite and cavitate. This means losing power, especially when backing. If the stern is low and the bow high, then the wind will push the bow when trying to maneuver, and the captain must compensate. If a twin-screw tug suffers minor damage to a propeller (usually from logs or other floating debris), the captain may have to balance the engine speeds to get a good "head on" push. (If the propeller is badly damaged, it will cause a horrible vibration and must be repaired). Many small items may have an impact on a tugboat's handling characteristics, and a good captain will recognize and compensate for them.

Once a captain has a complete understanding of his own craft, he must judge how the ship being worked will react. The length, draft, and height of ships vary, and as a result all ships will handle a bit differently. And just as the weight

Often when a tug is working alongside a ship, helping it dock for instance, a headline is run from the bullnose on the tugboat to a cleat on the ship. The tug can push against the side of the ship to move it one way, or can pull back against the line to move it in the other.

distribution influences how a tugboat handles, it affects how a ship handles. If the ship is more heavily loaded on the stern, and light in the bow, the ship will pivot at a different point than it would if it were equally loaded.

Once the captain has a handle on his own craft and the one to be assisted, he must anticipate how the elements will affect both their tugboat and the ship or barge being moved. Wind can be a huge factor in a captain's decision-making process. The typical barge or ship presents a massive "sail area" for the wind to push against. The taller and wider a barge or ship is, the more air it will catch, just as a side wind will sway a Chevy van more than it will a

Working in tight quarters around large ships, a tug's maneuverability really pays off. By moving quickly from one part of the ship to another, the tug never leaves the ship unattended for more than a short time. This keeps wind and current from disturbing the ship's maneuvering pattern.

Corvette. A heavily laden vessel will sit deeper in the water and present less of its bulk to the wind than an empty ship with more of its sides above water. And winds can have the nasty habit of shifting. A captain may have to compensate for a change in wind speed or direction during the middle of a maneuver.

Currents will also have a tremendous effect on which way a ship or barge moves. A full ship with its hull sitting deeper in the water will be more affected by current than a ship that is empty. If a ship is trimmed so the bow is light and the stern is heavy, it will change the handling characteristics of the ship. The stern, which is deeper in the water, will be more affected by current than wind. The bow, mostly above the waterline, will be less influenced by current but more prone to wind movement. Captains must gauge the strength of both wind and current and their effect on the type of craft they are assisting, and anticipate these factors throughout the maneuver. When working with the wind and current going in the same direction, there is often no second chance; a mistake may result in ship damage, dock damage, or worse.

When working at night or in rain, fog, sleet, or snow, a captain must be competent working with limited visibility. He must be proficient at radio communications, radar use and interpretation, GPS systems, and (here's the good bit) must be able to do the same job without them. Competency in chart reading, compass work, and celestial navigation is as prudent knowledge for mariners today as it was 200 years ago. The reason is obvious. While radar and GPS systems are wonderful, they can break. A captain must be able to do it the "old" way just in case some or all of the hardware fails.

As soon as a captain has a handle on all of the physical factors affecting the job, he is

Often a docking job requires two or more tugboats. During these maneuvers, the tugboat captains take commands from the port's pilot. The pilot is quite familiar with the local waters and conditions and is like an orchestra conductor, giving commands to all vessels involved.

ready to move something. While every tugboat job is somewhat different, most all of them fall within the five basic ship-handling maneuvers. These are propelling, steering, turning, moving a vessel laterally, and checking a vessel's way. These are the five things that ships and barges find difficult to do on their own in tight quarters, and thus they call a tugboat.

Before the actual ship-handling maneuvers begin, the tugboat will most often come close alongside the ship so the ship's crew can pass lines to the tugboat crew. When coming alongside, a tugboat will position itself parallel to the ship. When the ship is dead in the water this is easy to accomplish, and the captain will maneuver his boat alongside the ship just as he does when he docks. However, when the ship is moving, coming alongside becomes more difficult. The captain will first approach the ship on a parallel course. As he closes in he will match the ship's speed. When he has the tugboat moving at the same speed as the ship, he will move closer to the ship. Where he intends to come alongside the ship will dictate his maneuver. Approaching toward the bow is easier and less dangerous. The bow wake of the ship will most likely push the tugboat away, and the tug captain will have to turn in toward the ship to compensate. However, when approaching toward the stern, or "on the quarter," there may be a suction effect placed on the tug, tending to pull it into the ship. In this situation the captain must steer away from the ship to keep the tug from being sucked in. This can be terribly

A ship will come into port on her own as far as is possible. This varies from port to port, depending on the available room to maneuver and hazards to navigation. The ship will have radioed ahead to inform the tugboat company of its arrival.

dangerous, as the propellers (big, mean 30-foot-tall propellers) of many ships are exposed above the waterline when they are sailing without cargo. Once the tug is alongside, it is time for the maneuvers to begin.

Propelling

Propelling is, by its simplest definition, providing engine power. This may be used in conjunction with ship's engines, or a pilot may use the tug alone for power. Propelling is usually accomplished by using a towline run from the front of the ship to the back of the tugboat. Typically, the line is 100 to 150 feet in length. However, when working in tight quarters, the line will be brought in and will be shorter. The shorter the towline the more danger to the tug.

A tug with a ship on the line is like a man with a horse on a line. As long as the horse behaves all is well, but if the horse gets out of control, the man on the line is in trouble. The same is true when a tug has a ship on a line. If the towline cannot be released, the tug is at the ship's mercy. During towing maneuvers, the tug captain will often move to the doghouse to control his vessel. From here he can watch the ship, towline, and his crew to ensure control and safety. He will also keep one hand hovering around the line release control. This is the button that instantly allows the captain to let go of the horse.

Another technique for providing propulsion is "hipping up," in which the tugboat is securely lashed to the side (hip) of the ship, and the pilot uses the combined engines of

Securing a line from tug to ship is often the first maneuver in a docking. The tugboat will approach the ship and match speed. Once the tug and ship are moving at the same speed on a parallel course, the tug begins to move in toward the ship.

ship and tug to steer, in the manner of a twin-screw boat. A pilot can run the tug engine forward and the ship's engine backward to turn in one direction, or reverse his commands to turn in the opposite direction. This brings us to the second function of tugboats.

Steering

Steering is assistance in providing directional control while a ship is moving, usually at low speeds. Ships often have to travel long distances in rivers, tight channels, and obstructed areas. They may use tugboats in conjunction with their own engines and rudders in order to make precise turns. As mentioned above, this can be accomplished by hipping up. A ship can also be worked with one tug in the front and one in the back,

both with a towline. Very precise and quick steering commands can be accomplished by using this arrangement.

Turning and Moving a Vessel Laterally

Turning is providing directional control while a ship is dead in the water. Moving a vessel laterally is used when a ship must move sideways with no movement forward or backward. Turning and moving a ship laterally will most likely involve maneuvers in which one or more tugboats push directly against the side of a ship with their bows. Where they push against the ship and how hard is more than a matter of guesswork. Each ship is different (unless they are identical sister ships), and because of this the tug captain's life is seldom routine. While the captain must be aware of the size, draft, and weight of the ship he his assisting, he must also recognize the pivot point of the ship. When a tug is pushing against a ship, the ship takes the role of a lever and the pivot point will determine how the ship turns.

I have made it a point throughout my life to stay away from advanced physics and mathematics whenever possible, and as a result I will not discuss the advanced physics and mathematics of moving a 90,000-ton ship with a 100-ton tugboat. However, a couple of common situations that we are all familiar with can illustrate the basic physics of ship docking.

The first principle is that of the pivot point. When moving a ship laterally or turning a vessel, it will rotate along its pivot point. The pivot point's location varies from ship to ship. It may also vary along the hull of a single ship, depending on the weight distribution of the ship's cargo. A simple example of this is a playground seesaw, which is nothing more than a lever balanced on a fulcrum, just like a ship. If two 100-pound kids get on each end of the seesaw, it will be balanced and remain level. This leaves the pivot point directly in the center of the board. However, if a 100-pound kid gets on one end and a 150-pound kid gets on the other, the side with the heavy kid will go to the ground, leaving the 100-pound kid high in the air. The difference in weight distribution has changed the pivot point. There are two ways to bring the seesaw back to level. The first, obviously, is to give the 100-pound kid a 50-pound bag of cement. The other way is for the 150 pound kid to slide about a third of the way in toward the fulcrum of the seesaw; then the board will come back to level. Just like seesaws, ships

Lines are thrown today the same way they have been over the centuries. A weight, either a sand bag or a "monkey fist" knot, is attached to a lightweight rope and thrown from one vessel to another. It is with this lighter line (around 3/8 inch to 1/2 inch in diameter) that the working line (2- to 3-inch diameter) will be passed.

have pivot points, and distribution of weight around a ship will determine the location of the pivot point.

Once the pivot point is understood, it's time to move on to how power application affects a maneuver. Our next example takes place in a living room. Let's say that husband and wife Bob and Carol are moving a couch and want to slide it from the center of the room straight back against the wall. Both choose an armrest at opposite ends of the couch and push. Bob (our first tug) is 6 feet 5 inches tall and weighs 250 pounds, while Carol (our other tug) is 5 feet 2 inches tall and weighs 110 pounds. If each pushes as hard as possible, Bob's side will slam into the wall before Carol's, because Bob is stronger. It's not much of a way to dock a couch. To prevent this, Bob may have to push at half strength and Carol at full strength to get an even movement, just as two tugboats do when sliding a ship laterally into dock. If they push with the same pressure on each end, the couch will slide directly back because the pivot point of the couch is in the center.

Now we can combine these two principles. What if Carol's mother-in-law (5 feet 6 inches tall and weighing 325 pounds) drops in and decides to sit on the couch while it is being moved. If she sat exactly in the center of the couch, the pivot point would not be changed.

Once the line is secured, the tug is ready to assist the ship. While proceeding to a dock, the pilot may use the tug to help with course corrections. With a gentle push against the hull or a pull on the line, the tug's assistance allows the ship to turn in a shorter distance than it can with its own rudder. This may be not only helpful but necessary when a large ship must move through tight, winding channels.

Turning a ship in is usually a matter of pushing and pulling. Pushing is accomplished by putting the nose of the tug directly against the side of the ship and giving the tug some throttle (above). The tug may push toward the bow or stern to pivot the vessel, or may push in the center or on the pivot point to move the ship laterally (below). If the tug pushes too far, or when the pilot wants to stop the pivot or lateral movement, the tug can counter the move by pulling back on the line (right). When the line is under this high a load, the smart deck hand will be inside the boat.

Even though there is more weight, the distribution has stayed the same. But needless to say, she will sit toward Bob's end. With the extra weight on the end, the pivot point will change. Bob's side will be heavier and, as a result, more difficult to push. Now, if they apply equal pressure, Carol's end will swing faster than Bob's. In order to push the couch evenly, Bob will have to push harder in order to keep up with Carol's side, or they can change their location on the couch, thus changing the amount of leverage. The maximum leverage is attainable at the end of the couch. Thus, if Bob stays at the end of the heavy side, Carol can move in a bit (just like the kid sliding down the seesaw). She will lose leverage, which means more pushing force is required, but this may allow for better control of the couch when moving.

While these examples are simple, they do demonstrate the basic physics that affect ships as tugboats try to turn them. Keep in mind that wind, current, rain, fog, rough water, and other variables of the sea were absent from Bob and Carol's living room.

Checking a Vessel's Way

Checking a vessel's way is the practice of using tugs as a braking mechanism to slow and stop ships. While this can be done with the ship's engine, it can be done with a greater degree of control using tugboats. A ship's rudder's efficiency is decreased in reverse, and as a result steering control is compromised. By using a tug, the ship can keep steering control and still be slowed.

In accomplishing these five functions of maneuvering, a captain may use many boat-handling techniques. Most involve directly pushing against the side of the ship, usually using the bow of the tugboat, or using lines run from the ship to the tugboat so that the tugboat pulls instead of pushes. Either way, these five basic maneuvers account for just about all of the activities that ship-assist tugboats perform. Without assistance in these areas, large cargo ships and tankers would not be able to safely maneuver in the tight ports that dot our coastlines.

And safety in these ports is very important. In 1947 in the port of Texas City, Texas, a large freighter caught fire. She carried everything from peanuts to bullets. Because of poor decision making in fighting the fire, and not towing the vessel out to sea immediately, two holds full of ammonium nitrate (fertilizer) aboard her exploded. This led to more fires and explosions in the port's other ships, refineries, and other manufacturing plants nearby. A week later, when all of the fires were finally put out, over one-third of the town of Texas City was destroyed and 581 people had died. While this accident was not the fault of a tugboat, it does underline how important procedure and safety are when handling ships in port. This applies not only to the ships and crews, but also to the residents of all of our port cities.

As time goes on there will be more and more advancements in the technology of tugboats. As there have been in the past, there will continue to be refinements in hull shape and engines, and layouts will continue to be made. But it won't change anything. The facts are that the physics of working the ships and the grit of the tugboat crews cannot, and will not, be improved. They are the basis of ship assist, and regardless of the craft sailed, it is these attributes that will ensure the future of the tugboat.

Glossary

Abaft: At the rear of a vessel, toward the stern.

Abreast: Even with, or side by side, as, "We'll come abreast of the other vessel."

Aground: When the keel, or underside of a vessel, is stuck on the bottom, she is aground.

AWO: The American Waterways Operators, a leading national advocate for the tugboat, towboat, and barge industries.

Beam: The width of a vessel at its maximum.

Bow: The forward part of a vessel.

Bull nose: A large, steel, ringlike fixture located toward the bow of a harbor tugboat. Lines are run through the bull nose, so that when tension is placed on the line, it will place the force on the centerline of the boat. It also keeps the line stable as the tugboat pivots.

Buoy: A floating marker used to show channels. They vary in size from 2 or 3 feet tall for river buoys to 10 to 15 feet for ocean buoys. The purpose of most buoys is to aid navigation, and a vessel stays between them to remain in the marked channel. Red buoys are on the right and green on the left when going upstream or returning into a port. (Remember: red—right—returning.) When traveling downstream or leaving port, the red markers will be on the left and the green on the right.

Capstan: A vertical winch located on deck, used to aid in bringing in lines.

Docking: A tugboat assisting a ship into port and to a pier, wharf, floating dock, or berth of any type.

Draft: The depth of a vessel's hull below the waterline. The draft of a vessel will vary depending on how heavily it is loaded. Even with the same load, the draft may vary depending on the seawater's salinity, which varies around the world.

Fender: A layer of material hung over the side of a vessel to protect it from impacts.

Freeboard: The distance between the waterline and the top of the deck.

H bitt: A large steel fixture on a tugboat deck that is used to secure lines. The name derives from the "H" shape of the bitt.

Hipping up: When a tugboat attaches to the "hip," or side of a barge or ship, it is said to be hipped up.

Pivot point: The vertical along which a ship rotates when pressure is applied to any point along her side. If the tug presses directly on the pivot point, the vessel should move laterally and not pivot.

Port: (1) The left side of a vessel. (2) An opening in a vessel for ventilation. (3) Shore installations that provide berthing and loading areas for ships and barges.

Reduction gear: A device located between the engine and the propeller shaft that reduces the rotational speed of the engine before power is transmitted to the propeller shaft. A 3:1 reduction gear will change the engine's 900 rpm (revolutions per minute) to 300 rpm for the propeller.

Scupper: Drain holes along the deck used to release seawater from the deck back to the sea.

Starboard: The right side of a vessel.

Stern: The rear portion of a vessel.

Index